Extraterrestrial Life

Look for these and other books in the Lucent
Overview series:

Extraterrestrial Life

by Richard Michael Rasmussen

LUCENT
B·O·O·K·S

LUCENT *Overview Series*

Library of Congress Cataloging-in-Publication Data

Rasmussen, Richard Michael.
    Extraterrestrial life / by Richard Michael Rasmussen.
        p.   cm. — (Lucent overview series)
    Includes bibliographical references and index.
    Summary: Discusses the possibility of life on other planets, what
conditions would support this situation, and how we are searching
for such life-forms.
    ISBN 1-56006-126-X
    1. Life on other planets—Juvenile literature.   [1. Life on other
planets.]   I. Title.   II. Series.
QB54.R37   1991
574.999'2—dc20   91-15564

Contents

Introduction

THE EARTH ORBITS in a universe so large it is difficult to imagine that we are its only inhabitants. Our own galaxy consists of several hundred billion stars, and it is just one of a hundred billion other galaxies in the universe. Within these galaxies, perhaps, are untold numbers of stars, planets, pulsars, quasars, black holes, and more. And somewhere out there in the cosmos, many scientists believe, other living beings must also exist.

Human beings have long toyed with the idea that they are not alone in the universe. Such thoughts brought great personal hardship to those who spoke openly of them early in human history. Yet these ideas, fanned by human curiosity and advances in technology, failed to disappear. Many years passed before human beings developed the tools to seriously search for signs of extraterrestrial life, or life-forms from other worlds.

The search finally took shape in the mid-twentieth century and has continued to the present. The core of modern efforts lies in telescopes that detect electromagnetic energy coming from space. These telescopes pick up the sounds of the universe and record their patterns for later study. Even with the advanced equipment available today, this is no easy task. As with any venture into the unknown,

(opposite page) A Martian craft hovers near the earth in an illustration that suggests there might be other life in the cosmos.

7

The search for extraterrestrial life includes the use of radio telescopes. Radio telescopes detect the electromagnetic energy generated by stars and other celestial objects.

the search for extraterrestrial life has experienced highs and lows and taken many false steps. Occasionally, as happened in 1967 in England, the search for extraterrestrial beings has led scientists in unexpected but exciting new directions.

"Little Green Men"

English astronomers were using a special kind of telescope to explore the heavens. This instrument, known as a radio telescope, detects a type of electromagnetic energy called radio waves. Radio waves are generated by stars and other natural objects in space as well as by human activity on earth. If other civilizations existed, their activities probably would also generate radio waves. So, scientists follow these waves in hopes of finding extraterrestrial civilizations. While studying telescope records at Cambridge University, student assistant Jocelyn Bell noticed something highly unusual. The records showed a pattern of steady, brief pulses. These signals were much different from the irregular pulses normally recorded. Bell showed the records to university astronomers.

The astronomers grew excited at her discovery. Information indicated that the signals were coming from a very small object in the sky. The steady pace of the signals suggested that there was some sort of purpose or intelligence behind their origin. It was entirely possible, thought the scientists, that the signals were from an extraterrestrial source, perhaps intelligent beings on another world. The astronomers hastily named the unknown source LGM-1, for "Little Green Men."

Further study of the patterns seemed to indicate that what Bell had discovered was not a message but some sort of interstellar beacon. This signal was just the kind that an alien civilization might use to guide starships through space. Soon, other radio observatories joined in monitoring the beacon. As they did so, scientists realized that Bell had indeed stumbled onto an incredible new discovery. The signals were not coming from an alien spacecraft, however. They were instead coming from a bizarre natural object deep in space. Bell had discovered a pulsar, or pulsating star, which produces a burst of radio waves, or signals, each time it rotates. The existence of pulsars had long been suspected. But until Bell's discovery, the existence of these rapidly rotating stars had not been confirmed.

Scientists were disappointed by the false alarm over detecting an intelligent signal but were excited by the pulsar discovery. The designation LGM was quickly dropped. Meanwhile, efforts to find signs of extraterrestrial beings continued. One of these presented a classic example of the difficulties scientists faced.

Mistaken identity

In the early 1970s, a team of Soviet scientists began a deliberate search of the sky for intelligent signals. It was not long before they reported some results. On October 16, 1973, the Soviet news agency Tass reported:

> Samuil Kaplan, director of the Radio Institute of Gorky, has announced the reception of signals of an unusual nature. . . . The signals . . . are repeated over a wide range of wavelengths. . . . The possibility of these signals being of extraterrestrial origin cannot, at this stage, be completely ruled out.

A month later, a top Soviet space scientist, Dr. Vsevolod Troitsky, also commented on the signals. He said, "They are definitely call-signs from an extraterrestrial civilization. This is only the beginning of some very exciting discoveries."

A colleague, Dr. Nikolai Kardashev, added, "We have been receiving radio signals from outer space in bursts lasting from two to ten minutes. Their character, their consistent pattern, and their regular transmissions leave us no doubt that they are of artificial origin. That is, they are not natural signals but have been transmitted by civilized beings with sophisticated transmission equipment. We can say the source is located in our own solar system."

Kardashev believed that the signals were coming from a spacecraft that had entered earth's solar system. But scientists around the world were skeptical, especially after the LGM experience. Eventually, the Soviets confirmed that the signals were indeed coming from a space probe. But the probe was not extraterrestrial. It was merely a U.S. military satellite. Again, the world was disappointed over the false alarm.

Tremendous possibilities

During those brief moments, however, when scientists thought they were actually receiving signals from other worlds, they were excited. It was breathtaking for them just to consider the possibility that contact had taken place. The benefits of such a discovery would be tremendous. Civilizations hundreds, thousands, or millions of years more advanced than earth's might have much wisdom to offer. Possibly, such a civilization could help unravel the many mysteries that have puzzled human beings since they first began to think and reason. Such a discovery might even help earth's population better understand itself. Dr. Thomas McDonough, an astrophysicist, author, and coordinator of extraterrestrial research, says:

> The greatest benefit would just come from knowing that there is another civilization out there. Right now, without that knowledge, we tend to think of ourselves as being unique in the universe, and [that] people in one culture . . . are special and very different from people in another culture. So the Russians, the Chinese, and the Americans all think of themselves as being very different from

The Milky Way galaxy contains more than 100 billion stars.

one another. But if suddenly we had positive proof that there were some two-headed little green men in another world with a more advanced civilization, we would begin to see ourselves as a single species in which our differences were trivial compared with the differences between us and them.

Most people agree that the detection of life on other worlds would represent one of the greatest events in human history. It could even represent a turning point for humanity. Whatever the results, it is an idea worth considering because it is entirely possible that we will make contact within our lifetimes. Today, scientists are actively searching the skies for intelligent signals, watching for the one discovery that will not be a false alarm.

1

Is Anyone Out There?

SINCE THE DAWN of recorded history, humans have looked to the stars and asked, "Is anyone out there?" It is a question that has been asked repeatedly by virtually all cultures of the earth. Thus, it is a question that has been addressed, and sometimes answered, many different ways.

Over this long period of time, humans have gradually grown to accept the idea that there might be life on other worlds. But it was not always this way. There was a time when the earth seemed to be the only world in the universe and its inhabitants the only beings.

Many ancient peoples described the heavens as a solid canopy, enclosing a flat earth on all sides. The stars were merely pinpoints of light, and the sun and moon were lamps to light the earth. To these ancient peoples, there was little else to the universe. The only "extraterrestrials"—beings living beyond the earth and its atmosphere—were a variety of gods and demons thought to populate the limited space beyond the canopy.

(opposite page) Many ancient peoples believed the heavens enclosed the earth and that they were the universe's only inhabitants.

The ancients had little other than the moon and the sun for supposing that there might be other worlds. But in 400 B.C., the Greek philosopher Metrodorus of Chios speculated that there might

Aristotle believed the sun, moon, and stars all revolved around the earth. His geocentric theory was accepted widely for two thousand years.

be other worlds, and other life. He wrote, "It is unnatural in a large field to have only one shaft of wheat and in the infinite universe only one living world."

Earth's place in the universe

However, it was the thinking of the Greek philosopher Aristotle that most heavily influenced the scientific reasoning of Western societies, beginning around 345 B.C. A wise man in many subjects, Aristotle thought that the earth and the humanity living on it were the center of the universe. He said that the moon, sun, and stars all revolved around the earth. In this geocentric, or earth-centered, universe there was no allowance for other beings or other worlds. The earth was unique in all creation, and humanity held a supremely important place in the universe. Indeed, with humanity the sole focus of all purpose, there was no need

Ancient symbols of the sun, moon, stars, and heavens revolve around the earth in this illustration.

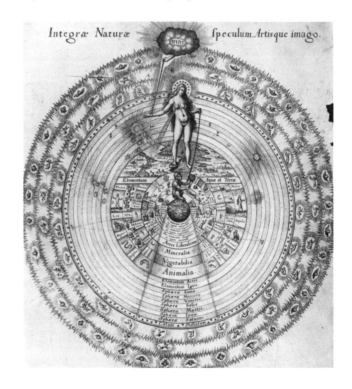

for other worlds or other beings.

People put such faith in Aristotle that his teachings were accepted as truth by many. Although others, such as the second-century B.C. Syrian writer Lucian of Samosata, wrote stories about other worlds and intelligent beings on the moon and sun, Aristotle's views dominated for a period of two thousand years.

No one seriously challenged the earth-centered system until the early sixteenth century when the Polish astronomer Nicolaus Copernicus promoted a heliocentric, or sun-centered, concept. Copernicus correctly said that the earth circled the sun. This was a revolutionary change in thinking because it reduced the earth to a less important role in the order of the universe. Humanity was no longer the center of all creation. The implication of this idea was clear: If the earth was no longer special, then other worlds could be circling the sun too.

Watching the planets

The ancients were also well aware of the planets. But they knew them only as pinpoints of light in the sky, different from stars only in that they seemed to change position from one night to the next. Up to this time, no one really knew that the planets were other worlds. But between the years 1609 and 1610, when Italian astronomer Galileo Galilei aimed his pioneering telescope at the planets, it became obvious they were much more than mere pinpoints of light. His discovery of lunar mountains and craters, rings around Saturn, and moons orbiting Jupiter all indicated that the planets were other worlds. Even though church doctrine at the time did not acknowledge Galileo's discoveries, other scientists realized their importance. They knew that where there were other worlds, there could be other life. But

With his telescope, Galileo saw mountains and craters on the moon, rings around Saturn, and moons orbiting Jupiter.

Johannes Kepler believed intelligent beings built the moon's craters and lived inside of them.

few, including Galileo, were willing to state this possibility openly.

One of the first scientists to do so was the German astronomer Johannes Kepler. Kepler said that intelligent beings lived on the moon, and as evidence he cited Galileo's observation of a large circular feature on the moon's surface. This feature, later identified as a crater, was built, Kepler said, by intelligent beings who "make their homes in numerous caves hewn out of that circular embankment."

Writers of the time were quick to pick up on the idea of life on the moon. In 1638, English clergyman Francis Godwin penned a story called *Man in the Moone*. The story's hero flies to the moon in a chariot pulled by migrating geese. There, he discovers a world much like earth. In 1650, the French poet Cyrano de Bergerac published a story called *Voyage to the Moon*, in which the hero discovers the moon to be populated by intelligent beings. These stories were quite popular with the public and kept alive the notion that life might exist on other worlds. Even the English astronomer William Herschel, famous for the discovery of Uranus and his studies of stars, was caught up with the idea. He suggested to other astronomers that there might be life on the sun, an idea later shown to be incorrect.

Creatures on the moon

The public was so taken by the idea of life on other worlds that it was willing to believe almost anything. One man, English journalist John Locke, thought the whole idea of life on other worlds was silly and decided to take advantage of the public's willingness to believe. He authored a sensational series of newspaper articles in the New York *Sun*. These articles described startling new discoveries by Herschel's son, John Herschel, who was also an astronomer.

With blazing headlines, the newspaper announced in its August 25, 1835, issue that John Herschel had detected life on the moon. This and subsequent stories described the moon as an earthlike world populated by flowers, trees, lakes, animals, and intelligent creatures. The newspaper printed drawings of some of the creatures, who resembled winged apes. It said they had "short and glossy copper-colored hair" and "wings composed of thin membranes." Additionally, the article said, creatures were observed gesturing with their hands, as if talking. This activity, according to the article, was evidence "that they were rational beings."

The city of New York, and soon the nation, was buzzing over the articles. People rushed to read the stories, briefly making the *Sun* the hottest-selling newspaper in the world. John Herschel did not share the public's fascination with these stories. He told reporters that he knew nothing of these so-called discoveries and had never seen any creatures. Besides, he said, astronomical discoveries had revealed the moon to be a rocky world without air or water—a hostile, lifeless world—hardly a home for exotic moon creatures.

Controversial claims

Astronomers soon exposed the series as a hoax. Despite the hoax, some scientists maintained an interest in the idea of extraterrestrial life. They turned their attention from the moon to the planets, where, they thought, there was actually the hope of finding an inhabited world. One scientist in particular, American astronomer Percival Lowell, carried this pursuit to an extreme degree. His controversial claims would influence the thinking of the public and some fellow scientists for nearly one hundred years.

The New York Sun *reported that astronomer John Herschel had detected an earthlike world existing on the moon. Although Herschel denied the story, the idea caught on that life might exist elsewhere.*

In 1877, Lowell pointed his telescope toward Mars. He was in search of strange markings on the surface. An Italian astronomer, Giovanni Schiaparelli, had reported seeing these markings. He called them *canali*, which is Italian for channels. Lowell, in turn, interpreted this to mean canals and was fascinated with the idea of canals on Mars. He decided to study the idea further. Thus began a quest that would fire the imaginations of astronomers, writers, and the general public for a long time to come.

Telescopes at the time revealed the blood-red planet as a fuzzy image with dark patches that seemed to change in size and shape with the Martian seasons. The dark areas were thought to be vegetation, and the light areas, desert sand. Lowell strained to see details in the fuzzy images. When he looked, he saw faint lines crossing the areas between the patches. He assumed these were the great canals, constructed by a race of intelligent beings. In the Martian summer, thought Lowell, the canals brought water from the melting polar ice caps to the desert and distributed it to the patches of vegetation. This seemed evi-

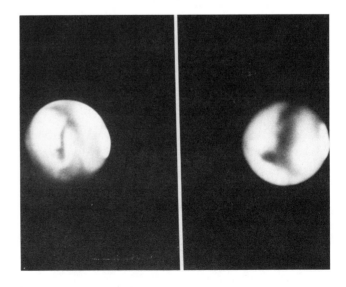

Initial observations of Mars revealed a planet covered with dark patches that seemed to change shape with the seasons. Faint lines between those patches were thought to be canals built by intelligent beings.

dence enough that Mars was populated by beings much like ourselves.

Lowell drew numerous maps of the canals and wrote extensively about his theories. In one of his books, *Mars as the Abode of Life*, he described what he saw through his telescope:

> The great number of lines form an articulate whole. Each stands jointed to the next in the most direct and simple manner—that of meeting at their ends. . . . It resembles lace-tracery of an elaborate and elegant pattern, woven as a whole over the disk, veiling the planet's face.

Many astronomers studied Lowell's maps and turned to their own telescopes to search for the canals. Some reported seeing them and drew their own maps. Others could not see the canals at all. Thus not all astronomers were convinced they existed.

Some scientists said that even if the canals were real, they would not be visible from earth. Lowell addressed this problem in his book *Mars*, published in 1894. He explained that the canals were visible from earth because of strips of vegetation growing alongside them. The strips, he said, made the canals easier to spot.

Camille Flammarion believed a great civilization had built the Martian canals. People wondered if that same civilization could communicate with earth.

Communicating with earth

The French astronomer Camille Flammarion was one who supported Lowell's views. In 1892, he published a book called *The Planet Mars*, in which he too argued that a great civilization had built the canals. He also wondered if it was possible that this civilization would find a way to communicate with the earth.

Two radio pioneers, Nikola Tesla and Guglielmo Marconi, also wondered if Martians might be trying to communicate with earth, perhaps by using radio signals. In 1901, Tesla noted that he had received some strange signals on one

Nikola Tesla thought the odd signals his radio received in 1901 originated from Mars or Venus.

of his radio receivers. The signals were unusual in that they seemed to come from outer space and followed a pattern that indicated they were possibly artificial in origin. Tesla thought that Mars or Venus was the likely source of the signals.

Marconi said that he, too, had detected unusual radio signals. The signals lasted much longer than those of any known earthly radio sources. For that reason, he thought they might have come from Mars. In 1922, when Mars was at its closest approach to the earth in some years, Marconi put to sea with a "floating laboratory" in hopes of picking up clearer signals. The June 16, 1922, issue of the *New York Times* reported that, after a month at sea, Marconi had "no Mars message yet," and would "have no sensational announcements to make."

Though no one could really prove that the signals had come from Mars, these reports served to convince others that the planet was a possible home for living beings. This possibility took on a new reality in the minds of many Americans on October 30, 1938.

The night the Martians invaded

Listeners tuning in that night to a CBS radio network show heard a startling announcement. Martian invaders had landed at Grovers Mill, New Jersey, and were engaging U.S. military units in ferocious battle. As the show progressed, bulletins and on-the-spot reports continued to pour in. Martians were landing everywhere. Thousands of people were being killed by deadly heat rays and poisonous black smoke. Whole cities were on fire. The Martians were destroying everything in their way.

Listeners across the nation panicked. Some fled their homes, covering their faces with wet handkerchiefs for protection against the poi-

sonous smoke. Others raced off in their cars, trying to escape the advancing Martian armada. Still
others sought refuge in churches. Police stations
and military installations were swamped with
calls. Hospitals treated people for symptoms of
shock and hysteria.

The radio broadcast was actually nothing more
than a dramatic re-creation of a novel written
forty years earlier by a British science fiction
writer named H. G. Wells. The Wells novel,
called *War of the Worlds*, told a tale of scientifi-
cally advanced Martians invading earth. The pro-

*A death ray fired from an
invading Martian spacecraft
ignites a house on earth in this
illustration from H.G. Wells's*
War of the Worlds.

ducer of the radio dramatization, a young American actor named Orson Welles, made sure that announcements before and during the broadcast clearly stated that the program was a fictional account. But many people missed the announcements and thought the bulletins were real. Others were too excited or frightened to notice them.

The panic demonstrated the dramatic changes that had taken place in human thinking and the wide acceptance of the possibility of life elsewhere. It also demonstrated what could happen when people thought hostile extraterrestrials were invading. These were lessons that would be remembered decades later when scientists began planning for eventual contact with extraterrestrials.

Culmination of an idea

In the years following World War II, the public's fear of invasion by extraterrestrials increased when many people reported seeing strange objects in the sky, which they assumed had come from other worlds. They sometimes described these objects as flying saucers or unidentified flying objects, known also as UFOs. The reports seemed to have some merit when the U.S. Air Force formed Project Bluebook to investigate the sightings.

Between 1952 and 1969, Project Bluebook analyzed 12,618 sightings. The vast majority proved to have simple explanations. Only 718 remained unidentified. The project closed down in 1969 when the Air Force decided it could no longer "be justified on the ground of national security or in the interest of science." At about the same time, the University of Colorado finished a two-year study of UFOs, concluding that there was "no direct evidence whatsoever [that] any UFOs represent spacecraft visiting Earth from another civilization."

Although UFOs were never proved to be ex-

Thousands of people thought the War of the Worlds *broadcast, narrated here by actor Orson Welles, was a live report of an actual Martian invasion.*

traterrestrial in origin, they became the subject of many books and movies. For better or worse, the sensationalism over UFOs further imprinted the idea of extraterrestrial life on the minds of the public. Even today, many people confuse the subject of UFOs with the search for extraterrestrial life. In the minds of most scientists, however, the two subjects are completely separate. The chance of an alien spacecraft visiting earth is minimal, most scientists believe, given the enormous distances between stars and planets. For this reason, the search for extraterrestrial beings focuses on finding signals and messages beamed from other inhabited worlds.

As technology improved, scientists turned their telescopes past Mars to the other planets. But they simply saw similar fuzzy images. There was no conclusive evidence one way or another about the possibilities of life on some of these planets.

This led some scientists to study the conditions that would allow life to develop in the first place. If they could understand these conditions, they might be able to guess the likelihood of life on other worlds in our solar system and beyond.

By the 1960s, some scientists had studied these conditions enough to become convinced that the universe might be teeming with life. This conclusion represented the culmination of nearly twenty-four hundred years of speculation and introduced the new science of exobiology—a branch of biology concerned with the search for life outside the earth.

U.S. Air Force Project Bluebook staff study a UFO-sighting report. In seventeen years, they investigated and explained nearly thirteen thousand UFO sightings.

2

The Conditions
for Life

MOST SCIENTISTS BELIEVE that if life
exists elsewhere in the universe, it probably exists on planets much like earth, circling other
stars. These planets would have to provide the
proper conditions for supporting life. Not all
planets would be capable of this. In our solar system today, the earth appears to be the only planet
with the right conditions for widespread life. But
this does not mean that earth is the only life-bearing planet in the universe. Modern theory suggests that the universe holds many other solar
systems. And, many scientists say, there are
bound to be other life-supporting planets in some
of these solar systems. But scientists know little
about other solar systems. So they must look for
clues to the existence of other civilizations in
what they know about the formation of the earth
and the evolution of life on it.

Scientists believe that when the universe first
flashed into existence, it consisted mostly of the
elements hydrogen and helium. The first stars
were formed from these elements, but they were
too light to form life-supporting worlds. Over
time, however, nuclear reactions in these early
stars transformed the hydrogen and helium into

*(opposite page) The earth, seen
in this view from the moon's
surface, is the only planet in our
solar system known to support
life. Many scientists also believe
that conditions for life exist in
other parts of the galaxy.*

25

By studying the earth, scientists hope to find clues about the existence of life on other worlds.

heavier elements. Among these were the life-supporting elements carbon, oxygen, water, and iron.

When the largest of these early stars reached the ends of their lives, they exploded, spraying their elements into space. The newly distributed elements blended into a new, enriched mixture from which new stars would eventually form. These newer stars, and the planets around them, for the first time contained the mixture of elements necessary for life. This new mixture came together on earth like nowhere else in the solar system. Slowly, over millions of years, these elements combined to form the essential conditions for life as we know it. These conditions comprise certain chemical elements, water, light and energy, a hospitable climate, suitable gravity, and a protective atmosphere.

Life-supporting elements

Water and chemical elements such as carbon, metals, and minerals are present in all living matter. They are, in a sense, the basic ingredients of life. Carbon, for example, serves as a molecular building block, a sort of glue that binds together the molecules of living things. Carbon also allows living things to store energy, control activities within cells, and reproduce.

Metals and minerals are also important to life as we know it. The metal iron, for instance, helps form the hemoglobin that carries oxygen through our bloodstreams. The minerals calcium and phosphorus ensure healthy bones and teeth. Sodium chloride, or common salt, is a mineral that helps the body replace water lost through sweating.

Metals are particularly important to the development of an advanced civilization. In our case, we would not have cars, radios, televisions, or spacecraft without the availability of metals. And we would not enjoy the fruits of electricity and magnetism without them. A planet poor in metals would have little chance to develop life and virtually no chance of developing advanced civilizations.

Water is also vitally important to life as we know it. Most organisms on earth, including human beings, consist of about 50 to 95 percent water. The very nature of water makes it a critical part of the life process. For instance, it transports nutrients from one part of the body to another and provides moisture to cells. Many life-supporting chemical reactions take place in water. Without these reactions, essential biological processes such as digestion would not be possible.

Light and energy

Light and energy are also essential to living things. Life on earth gets its energy from the sun, radiated in the form of light and heat. Plants convert some of this energy to oxygen and store some of it for food through a process called photosynthesis. In turn, animals breathe this energy from the air and absorb it when they eat plants. Other animals take in these nutrients when they eat the plant-eating animals. Thus, energy from the sun supports the entire food chain on earth. Life elsewhere in the universe will also likely depend on a star for light and energy. It is important, however, that energy is present in the proper amounts. Too much energy, and radiation from the star would destroy the cells of plants and animals. Too little energy, and there would not be enough to support the food chain. To meet these conditions, a star must produce a moderate amount of energy at a steady rate over a long period of time, and it must live long enough for life to develop.

In the case of the earth, the sun has provided steady output for at least the last 3.5 billion years, the time during which life arose on earth. It is expected to remain steady enough to support life for at least that much longer. On the other hand, some stars experience drastic changes in energy output, turning "hot" and "cool" over extended periods of time, wreaking havoc on the environments of orbiting planets. Worlds around these stars are not likely to support life.

A chance for life

To allow a chance for life, a star must live a sufficient length of time. Some stars burn for about ten billion years, allowing plenty of time for life to develop on orbiting planets. But others, considerably larger and more massive than the sun, burn out quickly and die before life has a chance to develop. Or, they burn long enough for life to develop but die before intelligence evolves. This is because larger stars consume their fuels faster than smaller ones. For example, a star twice as massive as the sun will burn for only about one billion years. A star ten times as massive will burn for only about ten million

years. That is probably too short a time for any kind of life to appear.

A planet's climate is determined by several factors, including its distance from a life-giving star, its orbit around that star, and its rate of rotation. Just as is true in earth's solar system, a life-bearing planet must orbit its star at just the right distance. Too close, and the planet will be too hot for life. Too far, and it will be too cold. There is an area in between these extremes that is thermally habitable, or of suitable temperature for life. Only planets orbiting within the thermally habitable zone are likely to support widespread life. Within this zone, for example, water main-

A composite photograph of earth, Venus, Jupiter, Mercury, Saturn, and Mars. Of all these planets, earth seems to be the only planet capable of supporting life.

tains its liquid form long enough to provide moisture for the operation of life processes. Outside this zone, constant and extreme cold will cause water to freeze; constant and extreme heat will boil water until it evaporates into steam. Only a planet in the thermally habitable zone is likely to have liquid water in quantities large and constant enough to support life.

To remain within the thermally habitable zone, a planet must follow a fairly stable, circular orbit around its star, just as the earth does. If the planet follows a more elongated, or oval-shaped, path, it will pass in and out of the thermally habitable zone as it orbits the star. Such a planet will suffer extremes of boiling hot and freezing cold, making it unsuitable for life.

Another factor in determining climate is the rate of a planet's rotation. Earth, for example, rotates once every twenty-four hours, creating an

Plants are essential to life because they breathe in carbon dioxide and breathe out oxygen.

ideal split between night and day, leading to a balance in temperatures. This rate of spin also generates winds and weather conditions that are favorable for life. A planet that spins too fast will experience very short nights and days and suffer from ferocious winds and violent weather. A planet that rotates too slowly will experience excessively long nights and days, resulting in extremes of cold and hot. Such conditions would discourage the development of life.

A suitable atmosphere

Most scientists believe that life as we know it could exist only on a planet with a suitable atmosphere. An atmosphere provides an environment for weather, shields living things from harmful solar radiation, and provides gases for breathing. Without the atmosphere, various forms of weather, including wind and rain, could not distribute temperatures fairly evenly around the planet or transfer moisture from the oceans to the land. The atmosphere plays other important roles. A part of the upper atmosphere, the ozone layer, protects us from harmful ultraviolet radiation. Without this atmospheric protection, life would quickly die.

The atmosphere also provides the gases necessary for metabolism—the processing of matter and energy in living things. Life on earth is heavily dependent on the exchange of the gases oxygen and carbon dioxide. This exchange takes place between plants and animals. Animals, even those under the sea, breathe in oxygen and breathe out carbon dioxide. This alone would soon deplete the atmosphere of oxygen. Plants play an important role by doing the opposite—breathing in carbon dioxide and breathing out oxygen. Thus plants and animals are dependent on one another, replenishing the air supply for each other.

In its early history, the earth's atmosphere was likely very different from what it is today. Initially, it contained very little oxygen but probably had large amounts of hydrogen, ammonia, methane, and water. As they evolved, animals began the cycle of oxygen-carbon dioxide exchange. Because of this, the atmosphere changed over billions of years from one rich in hydrogen to one rich in oxygen. In other words, living things altered the atmospheric makeup of the entire planet. Exobiologists are interested in this fact for one reason. They believe that an atmosphere rich in oxygen does not exist without life. Detecting another planet with such an atmosphere would probably be a sure indicator of life.

Suitable gravity is another important factor in the development and support of life. Gravity exists everywhere. All objects in the universe tug and pull at one another. The degree of this pull is

Saturn has neither the atmosphere nor gravitational conditions needed to support life.

determined by the size of the objects and the distance between them. The gravitational pull decreases as the distance between objects increases. The sun's gravitational hold on earth is much stronger than its hold on Pluto, for example, because Pluto is so much farther from the sun. In general, though, the larger the object, the greater is its force of gravity. The smaller the object, the weaker its force. The sun is large enough to pull all of the planets in the solar system into its orbit, for example. In turn, earth is large enough to pull the moon into its orbit. But earth is not large enough to exert much gravitational force on any other planet.

The importance of planet size

Planet size not only affects the tug-and-pull between planets but also gravitational forces on the planets themselves. Giant planets, such as Jupiter and Saturn, have excessive gravity because of their enormous size. Objects on the surfaces of Jupiter and Saturn would be extremely heavy, and animals and people would weigh too much to even move around. The atmosphere, which is also held by gravity, would be so heavy it would crush anything on the surfaces of those planets if they had solid surfaces. Tiny planets, such as Mercury and Pluto, have very weak fields of gravity because they are so small. This weak gravitational pull is responsible for the relative absence of atmosphere on these planets.

The earth, of course, is the perfect example of a world with suitable gravity. Without it, the moon and atmosphere would drift off into space, and objects would float away from the earth's surface. All would be chaos. But, as it happens, the earth's gravitational force is strong enough to retain an atmosphere, yet not too strong to prevent the movement of people and objects on the

The atmosphere of the giant planet Jupiter would crush anything on its surface.

Gravitational pull causes planets and moons to align and orbit the way they do.

planet's surface.

Scientists think that finding a planet with the proper conditions would be a pretty good bet for discovering extraterrestrial life. Except for the earth, however, no such planet exists in our own solar system. Scientists have not thus far detected any planets outside of the solar system, but they believe they are there. They base this belief on a scientific concept known as the principle of mediocrity. According to this principle, the laws of nature relating to motion, gravity, energy, and other natural phenomena are the same everywhere. Therefore, the conditions that exist in one place must also exist elsewhere. This means that the earth is typical of a planet anywhere in the universe with life-supporting conditions.

Astrophysicist Thomas R. McDonough explains further. He says:

. . . When you look at the history of life on earth, and at what we're made of, there is nothing that seems terribly unusual when you compare the conditions on the earth with the conditions elsewhere in the universe. For example, the sun is not a weird star, it's not a rare star, it's one of the more common types of stars in the universe. Or if you look at what we're made of—carbon, hydrogen, oxygen, nitrogen—these atoms are not rare. If we were made out of platinum, for example, I might be worried about the basic ingredients of life being widespread, but we are made out of some of the most common atoms in the universe, ones that we have detected around distant stars and in other galaxies.

If this is so, then the earth and its inhabitants have evolved from common chemical elements, according to uniform scientific laws. If, as many scientists believe, these elements and laws are the same throughout the universe, then there is reason to believe that where conditions for life are right, other inhabited worlds also will exist. If this is true, the universe may be teeming with life. Many scientists think this is so and are now searching the skies for signs of extraterrestrial intelligence.

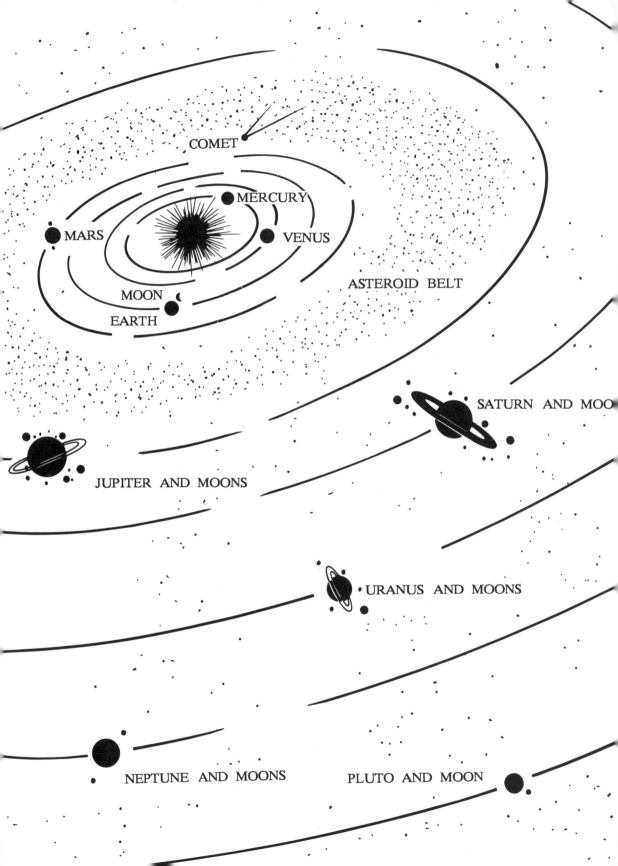

COMET

MERCURY

MARS

VENUS

MOON

EARTH

ASTEROID BELT

SATURN AND MOO

JUPITER AND MOONS

URANUS AND MOONS

NEPTUNE AND MOONS

PLUTO AND MOON

3

Looking for Life Elsewhere in the Solar System

UNTIL THE TWENTIETH century, human beings had no reliable method for detecting the existence of life on other worlds. People had only the fuzzy photographs taken from earthbound telescopes to study for signs of extraterrestrial life. But satellite space travel and other technological advances have made it possible for humans to explore the solar system close up for signs of life.

This search took shape in the 1960s and has continued to the present. Research during this time has shown the moon to be a harsh, airless world incapable of supporting life. Mercury, the closest planet to the sun, has neither air nor water and experiences temperatures of 648 degrees Fahrenheit in the daytime and minus-315 degrees Fahrenheit at night. Venus, named for the Roman goddess of love and beauty, offers a broiling, stifling atmosphere and 800-degree Fahrenheit surface temperatures capable of melting lead. The giant planets Jupiter, Saturn, Uranus, and Neptune seem unlikely homes for intelligent beings since they lack solid ground beneath their gas-

(opposite page) Satellite space travel and other technological advances of the twentieth century opened new views to the solar system.

The rocky, volcanic formations of Mars, shown in these photographs, led some scientists to believe the planet could support life.

filled atmospheres. Researchers know the least about Pluto, the planet farthest from the sun. But research indicates that Pluto is a frigid planet offering no chance for life of any kind.

The best hope for finding intelligent life in this solar system, other than on earth, seemed at one time to rest with Mars. But satellite photography and exploratory landings have shown that even Mars, with its earthlike rocky structure, polar ice caps, and atmosphere, is apparently barren of life. Most scientists are convinced that the canals and patches of vegetation that Lowell viewed as evidence of advanced civilizations were revealed as little more than optical illusions created by shifting sand and light.

Having given up hope of finding advanced civilization in earth's solar system, many scientists have shifted their focus. They have begun looking for signs of simple life-forms or conditions that might one day enable life to develop. Although less exciting in the short run, such discoveries would confirm the principle of mediocrity

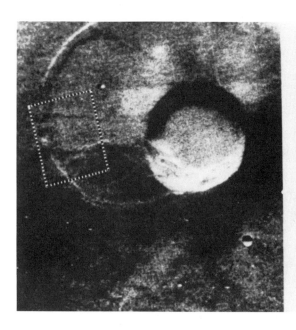

The surface of Mars, photographed by a camera on Viking 1, *consists of rocks, sand, and no vegetation.*

as well as the possibility that life is capable of developing anywhere in the universe if conditions are right. Three decades of searches for life in earth's solar system have brought mixed results. Some have led nowhere. Others have yielded fascinating but inconclusive results. Still others may yet determine the chances for some kind of life in other parts of the solar system.

Viking goes to Mars

In August and September of 1975, the National Aeronautics and Space Administration (NASA) launched two Viking spacecraft toward Mars. One of the mission's goals was to conduct experiments for signs of simple life in the planet's soil. The other goal was to further explore the planet's rocky surface for signs of ancient islands, rivers, and seas suggested by photographs taken earlier from space. The presence of water in the planet's past could be viewed as evidence that life—especially simple life—might once have existed on Mars.

On July 20, 1976, *Viking 1* landed in an area

An illustration depicts a Viking landing on Mars. One of the probe's tasks was to search for life-forms in Martian soil.

Experiments revealed a thin atmosphere on Mars, with little oxygen or water vapor and no sure signs of life.

called the Plain of Chryse. On September 3, 1976, *Viking 2* landed farther to the north, in an area named the Plain of Utopia. Both landers transmitted ground-level photographs and other information from their landing sites. The photographs and measurements revealed a cold desert strewn with rust-red rocks and boulders. Rust colored not only the sand and rocks on the ground but also the dust in the air, which accounted for Mars's red appearance. The landers also confirmed that the atmosphere was far too thin to support life as we know it. It contained very little oxygen and scarcely any water vapor. The only significant moisture was a little frost on the ground and a few thin, wispy clouds high above the planet's surface. Photographs detected no life-forms, not even primitive life-forms such as microbes, lichen, or moss that would have confirmed the existence of simple life on Mars.

In addition to taking photographs, each lander conducted the same three biological experiments. These experiments were designed to scoop the ground for soil samples and search the samples for primitive signs of life. Scientists were excited by the initial results. At first, all of the experiments seemed to show signs of biological activity. One such sign, the release of gases, could be evidence that microbes or similar organisms were alive and breathing in the soil. Ultimately, though, the test results proved inconclusive. The scientists decided they simply did not have enough information to know for sure whether Mars had ever supported life. "[The experiments] do not rigorously prove the existence of life on Mars," Viking biology team leader Harold Klein said after the mission. "They do not rigorously exclude the presence of life on Mars. My feeling is, we'll not be able to prove any more until we go back to Mars."

Evidence of an ancient civilization

Landers have made no return trips to Mars since the Viking missions. But other scientific efforts continued. One of these efforts, involving two computer scientists affiliated with NASA, even rekindled theories that advanced civilizations had once inhabited Mars. The two scientists, Vincent DiPietro and Gregory Molenaar, were interested in photographs of an area of Mars called Cydonia. In these photographs, taken from satellites orbiting Mars at high altitude, the two men identified what they believed were great pyramids and other structures suggestive of an ancient city. Science writer Richard C. Hoagland also saw the photographs and conducted additional studies. After completing these studies, Hoagland argued that the structures were indeed the remains of an ancient civilization. To support this conclusion, he cited a number of unusual surface features. Among the most interesting were features called The City and The City Square. In both regions, grid patterns similar to city streets

Writer Richard Hoagland studied photographs of Mars and found what he believes are the remains of an ancient Martian civilization.

could be seen along with pyramidlike structures in various sizes.

Hoagland also found other features in the photographs that reminded him of human civilization. One area, named The Fortress, seemed to have straight, towering walls and an interior section. Behind another structure, The Cliff, was an area of rugged terrain suggestive of diggings done by machines. There was also an inclined feature that to Hoagland suggested an access road. One of the most perplexing photographs revealed a giant rock structure looming upward in the unmistakable shape of a human face. Called The Face in the Rock, this structure measured one mile across and appeared to have sculptured into it eyes and eyebrow ridges, cheekbones on each side of the face, a mouth, and a chin. The face was somewhat Egyptian in appearance, according to Hoagland.

The features in the photographs confirmed the presence of an ancient civilization on Mars, as far

Hoagland contends machines dug The Cliff (left). The formation known as The Face in the Rock (far right) resembles a human face.

as Hoagland, DiPietro, and Molenaar were concerned. But NASA and other scientists disagreed with their conclusions. They attributed the structures to natural rock formations and to tricks of light and shadow. One scientist, Harold Masursky, argued that Hoagland's structures were nothing more than mesas, fractures in the ground, and natural formations worn down by the wind. Certainly, from the thousand-mile altitude of the photographs, it is difficult to tell. To this day, however, Hoagland, DiPietro, and Molenaar believe the structures in the photographs were built by an ancient Martian civilization.

Life-bearing possibilities

Although exploration of Mars and debate about its life-bearing possibilities continue, scientists have identified two other locations in the solar system that offer additional promise. One of these is Jupiter. At first glance, Jupiter seems an unlikely place for any kind of life. It is a truly enormous world, the largest of all the planets in the solar system and large enough to contain a thousand earths. Jupiter's "surface" is very different from the rocky world of the inner solar system. A thick raging atmosphere of orange-brown hydrogen and helium gases surrounds the planet. The atmosphere is whipped by ferocious winds into frigid cloud bands that race around the planet at 225 miles per hour. There is no solid ground to speak of beneath this atmosphere. Instead, scientists believe that the area beneath the planet's atmosphere consists of a warmer ocean of liquid metallic hydrogen.

Some scientists believe there is a region between this liquid hydrogen "ocean" and the cloud tops where conditions might be right for some forms of life. In this region, scientists have identified the presence of various substances including

Some scientists believe that life-evolving processes may be occurring in Jupiter's atmosphere.

methane, ammonia, and water. From these substances, life-forms may have already evolved. They are the same gases believed to have existed in the early atmosphere of earth and contributed to the formation of primitive life-forms. Therefore some scientists think that life-evolving processes might be taking place now in the atmosphere of Jupiter.

Envisioning life on Jupiter

Scientists have even come up with an idea of what creatures living in Jupiter's atmosphere might be like. They have no way of really knowing, but one idea envisions fishlike creatures floating up and down in the heat currents of this region. These creatures would have bodies shaped something like hot-air balloons. They could move about by forcing atmospheric gases through their bodies and wiggling their tails like fish. They would feed on the organic materials falling down from the upper layers of the atmosphere. They would spend their entire lives in this relatively tranquil region.

Scientists have conducted laboratory experiments to determine just how hospitable Jupiter's atmosphere might be to even simple life-forms. Through their experiments, they have found that microscopic bacteria could actually survive in an atmosphere like Jupiter's. These experiments offer some hope, but more work is needed. The satellite *Galileo* is now headed for Jupiter and NASA plans call for it to drop instruments down into the atmosphere of Jupiter in 1995. At that time, we should learn considerably more about Jupiter's atmosphere and the possibilities it offers as a home for life.

The other place in the solar system that has drawn special interest in the search for evolving life is Titan, the largest of Saturn's moons and the

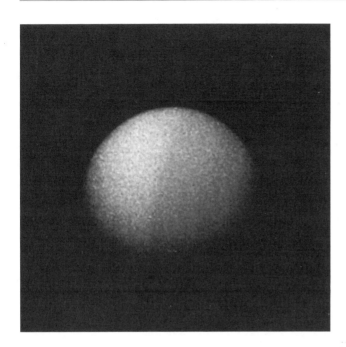

Saturn's largest moon, Titan, is of special interest to scientists who are searching for conditions in which life could evolve.

only moon in the solar system with a thick atmosphere. The atmosphere is so thick, in fact, that it blocks the moon's surface from view. The presence of the atmosphere in itself, however, improves the chances that Titan may play host to some of the conditions that precede the evolution of life. Exobiologists are especially interested because the atmosphere contains large amounts of nitrogen and methane, elements believed to have existed in the early atmosphere of earth. Indeed, some scientists believe that an "ocean" of liquid methane exists beneath the moon's atmosphere. This ocean of methane could play the same role that earth's ocean of methane did in its early history by providing a medium for the mixing of carbon-based molecules, a preliminary step in the long road to life.

Based on this information, it is conceivable that life-building chemical reactions, similar to those that started the process of chemical evolution on earth, may be taking place on Titan now. Perhaps

Titan will prove to be a living laboratory of planetwide proportions, where scientists may someday be able to study conditions similar to those that ignited life processes on earth three and a half billion years ago. NASA has plans to drop research instruments on Titan around the year 2002.

Searching between planets

While scientists mostly searched for primitive life on the planets of the solar system, a few still thought they might find signs of intelligent life between the planets. One such project was a search for alien probes—satellites or other robotlike vehicles sent from other worlds to explore earth's solar system.

In 1979, two scientists, Robert A. Frank Valdez, used a telescope to search for signs of spacecraft orbiting between the planets. They thought that such spacecraft may have been placed there to conduct ongoing observation of the earth and other worlds in earth's solar system. If this was the case, they reasoned, these spacecraft would need to be located where gravitational conditions would allow them to safely orbit for a long period of time. Mathematical calculations revealed two likely areas, one in the space between the earth and the moon, and the other in the space between the earth and the sun. These were the only two spots in the solar system capable of supporting stable orbits over long periods of time. The scientists took photographs through an optical telescope at Kitt Peak Observatory in Arizona and studied the photos for signs of alien probes. They did not find any.

It also occurred to some scientists that alien cultures might be mining earth's asteroid belt for the rich minerals and metals believed to exist there. The asteroids, a ring of rocks and boulders circling the sun, follow an orbit between Mars

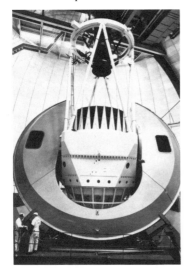

A telescope at Kitt Peak Observatory was used to search for signs of spacecraft orbiting between the planets.

The Infrared Astronomy Satellite is a heat-detecting telescope. Dr. Michael D. Papagiannis studied data from this telescope in his search for extraterrestrial life.

and Jupiter. One scientist, Dr. Michael D. Papagiannis, decided to conduct a search for such mining projects in the asteroid belt. His work with heat-detecting telescopes led to this idea. Most mining and industrial processes produce heat. So, Papagiannis thought, if mining colonies or industrial processing plants were out there, heat-detecting telescopes would detect them. To conduct the search, he studied data from the orbiting Infrared Astronomy Satellite, looking for hot spots indicative of artificially produced heat around the asteroid belt. He did not detect any signs of such activity.

These and other searches convinced most scientists that if they are to find other advanced civilizations in the universe they will have to look outside earth's solar system. There, in the outermost reaches of space, scientists have embarked on a search for intelligent beings.

4

Searching Beyond the Solar System

OVER THE LAST two decades, scientists have made many efforts to detect life beyond the solar system. This new, evolving field of science has become known as the Search for Extraterrestrial Intelligence, or SETI.

Because science has not yet developed an optical telescope powerful enough to see planets beyond our own solar system, most of the searches have depended on an instrument called a radio telescope. This instrument is not a telescope in the usual sense. It listens for noise rather than looking for light. Because radio telescopes hear farther than optical telescopes see, they are extremely valuable tools for searching solar systems beyond our own. By aiming a radio telescope at distant stars, scientists can listen in on the sounds of the universe or search for signals from extraterrestrial civilizations.

Detecting radio waves

These sounds are actually a form of energy called electromagnetic energy. Stars and many other objects in space naturally and constantly

(opposite page) An artist's view depicts the Pioneer 11 *satellite sweeping by Saturn. After searching the solar system, the satellite passed into deep space where its search for life continues.*

Dr. Bernard Oliver believes interstellar travel will never lead to human contact with extraterrestrials.

emit some form of electromagnetic energy. Manufactured objects also emit electromagnetic energy. Radio telescopes pick up one form of this energy known as radio waves. Radio waves, like other electromagnetic waves, are measured by their frequency. Frequency is similar in concept to the different stations on a radio or channels on a television. The person operating the radio telescope must tune in to a particular frequency to pick up radio waves. Unlike a typical radio or television, however, radio telescopes have millions of frequencies to choose from because radio waves actually travel in millions of different frequencies.

Radio telescopes pick up these waves with a dish-shaped antenna similar to the kind used to collect satellite television transmissions. The telescope's antenna focuses the radio waves into a concentrated signal so that they can be recorded and measured and their courses plotted.

Most scientists agree that radio signals are the most likely way to make contact with extraterrestrials because they offer the cheapest and most efficient way to communicate between stars. The distances between stars, and the time required to travel between them, would seem to rule out direct contact. Dr. Bernard Oliver, deputy chief of NASA's SETI program, says, "We are not going to make contact with the extraterrestrials by physical interstellar travel. Nor are they going to hop in their spacecraft and visit us. Not this year. Not this century. Not ever."

A subject for speculation

The early years of SETI research proved to be a struggle for the few scientists bold enough to work in the field. Many scientists saw SETI as a pseudo- or half science. To them, it was a subject for speculation and wishful thinking, not hard-core research. As a result, little time or money was spent on SETI by the scientific establishment during those early years.

The first straightforward effort at searching beyond our solar system for extraterrestrial life was conducted in 1960 at the National Radio Astronomy Observatory at Green Bank, West Virginia. The project director, Dr. Frank Drake, called the project Ozma after the princess in *The Wizard of Oz*. He chose this name, he said, because the land of Oz was "a place very far away, difficult to reach, and populated by exotic beings." In conducting this search, Drake hoped to detect radio signals from an extraterrestrial civilization.

Listening to the stars

At 4 A.M. on April 8, 1960, Drake aimed an eighty-five-foot radio telescope toward two sunlike stars, Tau Ceti and Epsilon Eridani. Each star was about eleven light-years from earth. (A light-year is the distance light can travel in one year at the speed of 186,000 miles per second.) With his telescope, Drake listened for anything that might appear to be an intelligent signal, such as a series of pulses or something to indicate a purposeful

Scientists at the National Radio Astronomy Observatory used these telescopes to conduct the first search for intelligent life beyond the solar system.

Frank Drake pointed a radio telescope toward two distant stars and heard a definite, patterned signal.

pattern. A recording pen would wiggle at the first sign of such a signal, and a loudspeaker would convert the signal into sound.

When Drake pointed the radio telescope at Tau Ceti, the pen immediately recorded a jagged line across a strip of paper, and the loudspeaker filled the room with the sound of static. But there was no pattern. So Drake pointed the telescope at Epsilon Eridani, and the pen, he says, went "off scale, *bang, bang, bang,* eight pulses a second." It was definitely a pattern.

Drake wondered if he had detected intelligent signals from a planet circling Epsilon Eridani. If so, this discovery represented a great moment in human history. Drake described his feelings at the time. "There's awe, there's elation," he said. "It's not a normal emotion. It's probably what people feel when they see what to them is a miracle. You know that the world is going to be a quite different place, and you are the only one who knows."

The signal vanishes

Drake adjusted the recording pen to make sure it was recording accurately, which it was. He then pointed the antenna away from Epsilon Eridani. The signal disappeared, just as he expected. When he pointed the telescope back toward Epsilon Eridani, hoping to find the signal again, the signal had vanished. Perplexed, Drake asked his technicians to aim the telescope away from the star again toward another part of the sky. The signals resumed. Drake then shrugged it all off, becoming convinced that the signal was generated by nothing more than a military surveillance plane flying overhead. He held out only the smallest hope that the signal was genuine: "It's still a possible candidate—it could be that Epsilon Eradani just transmits every hundred years for ten seconds or so." More likely, he added, "That was the biggest and best false alarm we've had."

Project Ozma continued for three months, scanning the skies for a total of 150 hours. No further unusual signals were detected. Though discouraged, Drake continued to believe that there were signals out there to be found. Although Drake's search found no evidence of extraterrestrial life, it inspired a whole array of SETI projects. Since Project Ozma, nearly sixty searches for extraterrestrial signals have been conducted in ten countries. The ten are the United States, the Soviet Union, Canada, Germany, Australia, France, Great Britain, the Netherlands, Japan, and Argentina. Between them, these countries have scanned the sky for about 200,000 hours. So far, these searches have detected no confirmed extraterrestrial signals.

One of the biggest challenges SETI scientists have faced, from the earliest days to the present, was figuring out which frequencies offered the most promise for detecting extraterrestrial life. With radio waves occurring in millions of different frequencies, narrowing the field of search was no easy task.

Exploring the water hole

Nevertheless, in 1971, scientists set about this task of deciding which radio frequencies alien civilizations would most likely use to transmit signals. Most researchers concluded that the most promising frequencies fell between the transmission bands of hydrogen (H) and hydroxyl (OH). The combination of these two elements represents water (H_2O). Thus this frequency range has become known as the water hole.

Scientists believe the water hole is an ideal place for detecting signs of extraterrestrial life for two reasons. First, water is essential to life as we know it. Thus the water frequency is a symbolic

This is the "wow" signal recorded at Ohio State University's radio observatory in 1977. The numbers represent the normal background noise of the sky, but the circled letters on the left indicate a very strong signal which could not be identified.

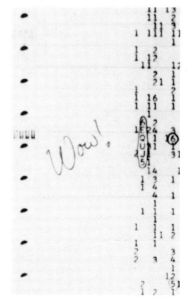

An unusual radio signal received in 1977 disappeared before Dr. Robert S. Dixon could determine its origin.

choice for any other beings who also depend on water for survival. Second, the water hole is an area of the electromagnetic spectrum that has a minimal amount of interference or noise from natural objects in space. Signals broadcast at this frequency would be fairly clear and easy to detect.

Because the water hole seemed such a promising place, some scientists decided to concentrate their efforts there. One important program began in 1973 at Ohio State University under the direction of Dr. John Kraus and Dr. Robert S. Dixon. This was the first full-time SETI project. The program is still active today, partially funded by NASA, with the rest of the money coming from volunteers and enthusiasts.

In 1977, the OSU telescope recorded an unusual pattern for a radio signal whose frequency was within the water hole. One of the scientists was intrigued enough by the signal to write "wow" in the margin of the printout. But just as the wow signal, as it has come to be known, got the attention of scientists, it suddenly stopped. Project scientists tried repeatedly to find the signal once more over a wide frequency range. They never again found it.

A signal from other beings?

Dixon was puzzled. The pattern of the wow signal did not match known patterns for earthly sources, low-orbiting satellites, or equipment malfunction. It could have been a secret military satellite, Dixon thought. Or, it could have been the hoped-for signal from other beings. "If so," Dixon said, "it seems that they were not trying very hard to attract our attention, since the signal disappeared before we could really find out what it was."

The OSU program has also detected some other unexplained signals. These have been received repeatedly, thousands of times, in pulses. Strangely, the signals have come from all over the sky and from different locations each time. This is strange because signals coming from an airplane, a satellite, or a distant civilization would come from a single direction. To date, no explanation for these signals has been found.

Excitement and disappointment

Despite the inconclusive results of the Ohio State University study, the water hole continued to intrigue scientists. They felt it offered one of the best chances for detecting radio signals from extraterrestrial beings, and so they continued to search in the water hole frequencies. Like the Ohio State study, later efforts would bring a mix of excitement and disappointment. At least one study, conducted between 1979 and 1981, provided just one more reminder of the difficulties the scientists faced.

During that time, a team of scientists led by Dr. Jill Tarter of NASA-Ames Research Center, observed 210 sunlike stars at water hole frequen-

This radio telescope at the Arecibo Observatory in Puerto Rico observed 210 sunlike stars. The telescope has also been used to study Venus and other planets.

cies. For this they used the Arecibo radio telescope in Puerto Rico. At one thousand feet across, the Arecibo telescope is the largest radio telescope in the world. The team also used a computer and new search techniques for a precise monitoring of possible signals.

The search picked up two "tantalizing" signals, Tarter said, stirring excitement among the scientists present. Additional analysis burst the bubble of excitement when tests showed that the signals had not come from outer space at all. Instead, they seemed to have come from a citizens band, or CB, radio in a car in the parking lot outside the research lab.

Scanning by the millions

Perhaps if more sophisticated equipment and search techniques had been available, scientists could have identified the false readings sooner.

This prototype of a Multi-Channel Spectrum Analyzer was built specifically for NASA's SETI project. The empty chair in the foreground symbolizes the system's automatic ability to detect signals from space.

Narrowing the searches to certain frequencies had helped, but the process continued to be slow and painstaking right up to the mid-1980s. Older equipment could focus on only one object at a time and scan that object one frequency at a time. With millions of stars to search and millions of frequencies available in the water hole alone, a tremendous amount of time and money would be required to conduct thorough searches.

If scientists scanned promising stars only at water hole frequencies, allowing just ten seconds for each frequency within that range, it would take about three hundred years to scan a single star, says astronomer Robert Jastrow.

During the 1980s scientists designed new equipment that considerably speeds up the process of scanning stars. The Multi-Channel Spectrum Analyzer (MCSA) is a computerized system enabling scientists to aim a radio telescope at a star and scan millions of radio frequencies at one time. Using this system, it would take only about a day to scan a star over a range of eight million frequencies. This allows scientists to scan many more stars in a much shorter time. Coupled with a radio telescope, the MCSA can monitor in thirty minutes a larger portion of the spectrum than have all previous SETI projects to this point. This kind of efficiency increases the chances of signal detection and reduces research costs tremendously. Invention of the MCSA was a key factor in getting Congress to fund NASA for a massive search for extraterrestrial life.

Searching for microwaves

In 1992, NASA is scheduled to launch the largest SETI project of all time. It will cover the wide frequency ranges in the microwave frequency window. This range of frequencies is relatively free of cosmic interference and includes the water hole frequencies. The search will scan more stars at more frequencies and at a faster rate than any searches to date. To do this, NASA is developing new MCSAs capable of scanning fifteen million frequencies simultaneously and across their full ranges. This will enable the instruments to measure larger frequency ranges. Scientists will connect the MCSAs to radio telescopes in the United States and other countries.

The new MCSAs will be more advanced in other ways too. They will have a sophisticated computer software program that will make it possible to recognize and reject radio interference caused by everyday sources such as microwave transmitters, aircraft, and automobile spark plugs. By easily rejecting common sources of radio interference, the NASA project hopes to avoid the kinds of false alarms that have plagued other programs in the past. The project will be largely automated. The system will require minimal operation by humans until a signal is received. At that point, the system will rapidly alert scientists that something unusual is at hand.

Two kinds of searches

The program will do two types of searches. The first is a targeted search that will concentrate on about eight hundred to one thousand specific stars, most of which are located within eighty light-years of earth. Scientists chose these stars because they had the characteristics needed to support earthlike planets. Each of these stars will be scanned for about a day. Researchers will be on the lookout for weak or stray signals from individual planets. It will take about ten years to complete the search.

The second search is a sky survey that will rapidly scan checkerboard patches of the sky. The survey objective is to look for incredibly power-

Edward Olsen of the Jet Propulsion Laboratory works on a project that determines if distant civilizations are transmitting radio signals.

ful beacons sent by distant supercivilizations. Such civilizations may have moved from their home planet to colonize a star system, using the beacons as navigational aids or forms of communication. It is "as if we were painting it with a big paintbrush," says Edward Olsen of the Jet Propulsion Laboratory (JPL) in Pasadena, California. The search, which will be conducted by NASA scientists at JPL, will last about five to seven years, scanning a wide frequency range. Additionally, it will scan ten thousand times more area than all previous SETI efforts together, and the instruments used will be three hundred times more sensitive.

NASA SETI scientists admit that the successful detection of an alien signal could take years— or it could come tomorrow. In our own galaxy, there are about 200 billion stars. Scientists believe we would have to scan about 200,000 of them just to have a fair chance of detection. Even then, the search may prove frustrating. Dr. Kent Culler, an astronomer and expert on signal searching, describes the work ahead as "searching the equivalent of the *Encyclopaedia Britannica* every second to find the part that says 'Hi, we're the aliens.'" He adds, "We will not by any means have surveyed the entire galaxy when we finish the ten-year search. This is the first step along what may be a very long road."

Beaming signals from earth

As scientists search the universe for signs of other intelligent beings, the earth's inhabitants unintentionally broadcast signals of their own existence into space every day. Radio programs, television shows, and military radar pulses are beaming outward from the earth in all directions. Moving at the speed of light, these signals have already passed hundreds of stars. Right now, radio

In this artist's rendition,
Voyager I *speeds through the*
solar system, past Saturn.

telescopes many light-years distant may be receiving old episodes of "The Lone Ranger" and "Leave It to Beaver," along with an endless stream of ads for soft drinks, soap, and deodorant.

Because of all these transmissions, alien radio telescopes would easily detect the earth. The existence of our civilization would be obvious. And yet, some scientists in the 1970s decided these unintentional messages were not enough. So they hit upon the idea of more purposefully announcing our presence in the universe. The reasoning behind this action was simple. If other intelligent beings live beyond earth's solar system, perhaps they too are searching for signs of life elsewhere in the universe. Why not help them find us?

Exploring the planets

In 1972, the United States launched two satellites, *Pioneer 10* and *Pioneer 11*, to explore the planets. These satellites are now headed out of the solar system into the deep void between the stars. The Pioneer satellites will continue into space for millions, even billions, of years unless they are captured by the gravity of another star. Each satellite contains a plaque depicting, with

Pioneer 10 *lifts off on its trip to*
Jupiter and beyond, carrying a
message for alien civilizations.

Voyager II *travels past Jupiter and is now beyond the solar system, heading into deep space.*

pictures and symbols, our civilization and location in the galaxy. Two other satellites, *Voyager I* and *Voyager II*, are also headed beyond the solar system with recordings of music, sounds, and language representative of the earth's population. The chances are slim that any of these satellites will ever be found by another civilization, but if they ever are, the beings of that civilization will learn of our existence.

We have also announced our existence by deliberately sending signals into space. In 1974, a group of SETI scientists, headed by Frank Drake, beamed a powerful radio signal toward the stars. Transmitted in binary code, the language of ones and zeros used by computer programmers, this message contains a physical description of ourselves and our planet and information about our location in the galaxy. This signal is still traveling toward distant stars. For better or worse, we have already announced our existence to the cosmos.

5

What Scientists Think About Extraterrestrial Life

IN A UNIVERSE filled with unexplored galaxies, each containing hundreds of billions of stars, it is easy to wonder about the existence of other civilizations. No one has yet found proof that such civilizations exist. The absence of proof, along with results from various studies, leads some scientists to believe that earth's inhabitants are essentially alone in the universe. But many scientists think the universe teems with life and that it is only a matter of time before we make contact with other intelligent beings. One scientist has even devised an equation for determining how many civilizations might exist and the chances of finding them.

Calculating the odds

This equation was developed in 1959 by Frank Drake, whose pioneering Project Ozma opened the doors to the modern search for extraterrestrial life. Drake believes that a universe containing as many stars as it does must be home to many intel-

(opposite page) Scientists have many different ideas about extraterrestrial life. Some envision human-like beings, while others imagine far different characteristics.

Frank Drake developed a mathematical formula to determine how many civilizations might be in outer space—and the chances of finding them.

ligent beings. His equation gives scientists a mathematical formula for predicting the likelihood of contacting other civilizations as well as determining how many civilizations might exist. To use Drake's equation, scientists make a number of estimates, including the number of stars in the galaxy, the number of stars that have planets circling them, the number of planets with intelligent life, and the number of civilizations that could avoid self-destruction. These estimates are then entered into the equation. Most of the figures are in reality unknowns, so scientists have to give their best educated guesses. As with all equations, the answer will depend on the figures put into it. Thus the equation does not provide any absolute answers, but it does give scientists a place to start in estimating the chances of making contact.

The equation is stated this way:

$$N = R. \times f_p \times n_c \times f_1 \times f_i \times f_c \times L$$

Each symbol represents a different factor that might influence the existence of life. One symbol represents the number of stars in the galaxy, for example. Another represents the number of stars capable of supporting life on a nearby planet. In this way, all the symbols in the equation are replaced with numbers based on the best information available. For example, scientists estimate that earth's galaxy contains 200 billion to 400 billion stars. So, a person using the equation would probably choose a number somewhere within that range.

Many communicating civilizations

Using his equation, Drake has concluded that earth's galaxy has many communicating civilizations. Other scientists have used the equation, too, and have come up with figures ranging from five hundred to one million communicating civilizations, depending on the numbers plugged into the formula.

Drake has also done other notable work in the SETI field. He has developed theories about what extraterrestrial beings would look like and how they would communicate. First of all, Drake believes extraterrestrials would be similar to us in appearance. He bases this belief on the assumption that the physical needs for aliens would be the same as they are for us. For example, they would probably have a head with a brain, eyes, ears, nose, and mouth all close together because it is biologically more efficient for these things to be arranged that way. They would probably walk upright on two feet because it is an efficient way to move around and frees other appendages (in human cases, hands) for manipulating objects. Extraterrestrial beings probably would have fin-

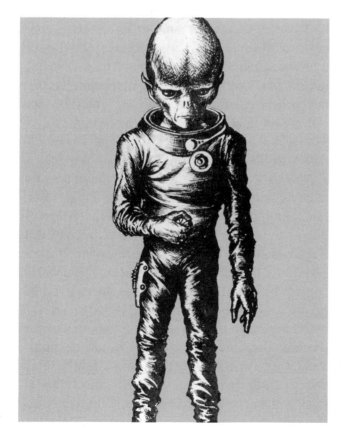

Drake and some other scientists believe extraterrestrials would look somewhat like humans. This caricature was drawn from details found in three hundred reports of UFO landings.

gers of some sort, although they might not have ten. Most aliens would look so similar, says Drake, that "if you saw them from a distance of a hundred yards in the twilight, you might think they were human."

Drake has suggested that advanced civilizations would use signals to transmit pictures. The pictures would serve as a sort of universal language that would be easier to understand than words. Thus the signal would be capable of translation by any intelligent civilization regardless of its language or method of communicating. Drake believes the pictures would be transmitted in binary code as a series of long and short pulses representing the black and white dots of a picture. At the receiving end, these pulses would be translated back into picture form. Even with this simple picture system, a large amount of information could be transmitted, including pictures of humans, molecules, numbers, and planets. Upon decoding, the images would be blocky in appearance, like the earliest video games, but they would be clear enough for intelligent beings to understand.

Alone in the galaxy

Not all scientists are convinced the universe is teeming with life. Physicist Frank J. Tipler of Tulane University of Louisiana in New Orleans is one of these. He believes that if extraterrestrials were out there, they would already have made contact with earth. Because there is no proof of contact by extraterrestrial beings, there is probably no one out there to visit us, Tipler believes. "I based my claim that we are alone in our galaxy on the idea that interstellar travel would be simple and cheap for a civilization only slightly in advance of our own. Thus if a civilization approximately at our level has ever existed in the galaxy, their spaceships would already be here. Since they are not here, they do not exist," Tipler says.

Biologist Zen Faulkes of the University of Victoria, British Columbia, Canada, is also skeptical about the likelihood of finding extraterrestrial life, but for different reasons. He believes SETI scientists are overoptimistic about the prospects of life evolving on other worlds. Faulkes believes there might be some life out there, although not very much of it, and very little if any with intelligence. This, he says, is because the evolution of life is probably a rare, rather than common, event. As evidence, he cites the earth's rocky road of evolution, characterized by what Faulkes describes as an unlikely series of lucky breaks, coincidences, accidents, and extinctions. Therefore, he sees it as highly improbable that evolution would take place on another world as it did on earth.

Supercivilizations throughout the universe

The search for extraterrestrial life has also created some strong believers. The Soviet astronomer Nikolai S. Kardashev is one of them, and he has some unusual ideas about the nature of extraterrestrial civilizations. Optimistic about the numbers of stars capable of supporting planets with life, Kardashev believes that the universe is home to numerous alien supercivilizations. Many of these civilizations, as Kardashev defines them, are highly advanced in science and engineering. He believes that the beings in these advanced civilizations may be more like machines than people because of their highly technical capabilities. This would be an electronics-based form of life instead of the carbon-based form found on earth. Such machine-life would have originally been created by living beings, Kardashev thinks. But the machines would have taken over for these living beings and even replaced them as they became more efficient at conducting

Nikolai S. Kardashev, standing behind a satellite model, believes numerous advanced civilizations populate the galaxies.

Kardashev believes the most likely place to find an advanced civilization is near the center of a galaxy. Pictured here is the Milky Way galaxy. In the foreground of the picture, a time-lapse exposure shows a communications satellite in orbit above the earth.

large-scale engineering feats. The machine-life would have the advantage of being able to work in space without special protection and to conduct engineering projects lasting hundreds or even thousands of years. Kardashev sees the transition from living beings to mechanized beings as the natural evolution of highly technical civilizations rather than as a case of one form of life intentionally wiping out another.

The most promising place to find these kinds of civilizations, says Kardashev, is toward the center of our own galaxy or the center of nearby galaxies, where the stars are older. In those locations, civilizations have had more time to develop advanced technologies. Kardashev even goes so far as to say that the cores of exploding galaxies might be evidence of meddling by advanced extraterrestrials. He offers this explanation in view of the fact that scientists have been unable to explain the natural forces causing such galaxies to explode.

Because supercivilizations would produce and use so much energy, Kardashev says, we might recognize them by the strength of their signals sent into space. The stronger the signal, the more advanced the civilization. The weaker the signal, the less advanced the civilization. Kardashev came upon this idea following his study in 1962 of a tremendous energy source detected at the far reaches of the universe. Although the source was later identified as a quasar, which is an exceptionally powerful yet compact object whose true nature is unknown, the study of this object suggested to Kardashev the idea that supercivilizations might produce energy of this magnitude.

Energy use may provide clues

Based on this notion, Kardashev came up with three groupings for civilizations. These groupings, based on the amount of energy a civilization might use, could be helpful, Kardashev thinks, in trying to understand the nature of an alien civilization. A Type I civilization, Kardashev says, is capable of using only the energy that reaches its planet from its sun. A Type II civilization collects and uses all the energy that its sun produces. A Type III civilization harnesses all of the energy produced by its galaxy.

A Type I civilization would be far more advanced than earth's population. Earth's inhabitants are not yet capable of using all of the energy that falls on the earth from the sun. This would separate a Type I civilization from our own. A Type II civilization might be one that constructs a gigantic sphere or shell around its sun to gather all its energy. Eventually, this civilization would develop the technology to travel between stars. It would probably conduct serious searches for life beyond its solar system. Additionally, it might attempt seeding other solar systems with life by launching spores or microscopic life-forms into space. A Type III civilization would expand throughout its galaxy. In so doing, it would tap the full energy of that galaxy. The technology of this civilization would be so great that it would

Kardashev's study of a tremendous energy source, later identified as a quasar, led to his theories of supercivilizations in space.

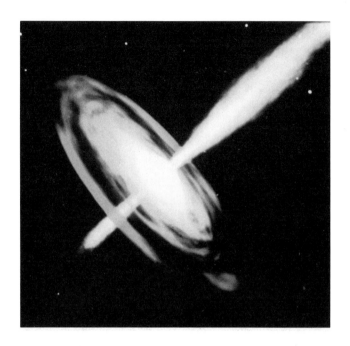

The energy emitted by black holes may be linked to the activities of advanced civilizations, according to Kardashev.

seem like magic to us. It might be capable of communicating in ways far more sophisticated than radio waves. Gravity waves, faster than light particles, and even some kind of mental telepathy might be the basis of their methods of communication. At current levels of human technology, earth's scientists might not even recognize these things as intelligent signals.

Kardashev believes there is probably only one supercivilization per galaxy. This, he says, is because a supercivilization would tend to gobble up lesser civilizations in its own galaxy. He concludes, "Many civilizations have been generated in our galaxy. But, immediately after contact, two civilizations combine, and as a result we have only one civilization, because there is big profit from combining the civilizations." He believes that after making contact with a civilization near the center of our own galaxy, for example, our civilization might be absorbed by the other.

To support his suggestion that supercivilizations exist, Kardashev points to unexplained, powerful radio signals emitted from the center of our own galaxy. Most scientists explain these signals as emissions from matter surrounding a black hole, a collapsed star where gravity is so strong that light cannot escape. Kardashev, however, believes this energy may actually be "connected with some kind of intelligent extraterrestrial activity" at the center of our galaxy.

A world among worlds

Other SETI scientists are not so outlandish as Kardashev in their predictions of what we might find. One such scientist is Dr. Carl Sagan of Cornell University, perhaps the most prominent spokesperson in the search for extraterrestrial life. Sagan cofounded The Planetary Society, a space-advocacy organization, produced the Public Broadcasting Service program "Cosmos," and has authored numerous books and papers supporting the search for extraterrestrial intelligence. One of those books, *Intelligent Life in the Universe*, coauthored with the Soviet SETI scientist I.S. Shklovskii, gave scientific legitimacy to the field at a time when it was severely lacking and launched unprecedented scientific interest in the subject.

Sagan firmly believes that the proper conditions for life are widespread throughout the universe and that there are probably a million civilizations more advanced than ours in the galaxy. Contact with another civilization, Sagan predicts, will be "an exhilarating and transforming experience."

Sagan, like many other scientists, accepts the notion that certain basic conditions must be present for any kind of life to exist. Those conditions can come together in many different ways, however. The mix of conditions on other worlds probably would result in beings who look and act very

Dr. Carl Sagan believes many advanced civilizations exist in the galaxy. He advocates continuing the search for extraterrestrial life.

different from earth's inhabitants, Sagan says. These differences, Sagan believes, will help unify the diverse populations and cultures of earth. The earth will no longer be a world of nations, but a world among worlds. "Whatever they are like," Sagan says, "the differences between them and us are going to be so much larger than the differences between any two human communities on the earth that SETI will necessarily have a unifying character."

Finding a common language

If and when extraterrestrials make contact with earth, Sagan is convinced that scientists will have no problem understanding their messages. Just as human scientists have searched for the clearest and most obvious means of communicating with other beings, other beings are likely to have done the same. Their search for a common language, Sagan says, will lead in only one direction. "There is a common language that all technical civilizations,

Sagan believes communication is possible between humans and extraterrestrials. Beside him is a model of Voyager II, *which is now carrying messages from earth to deep space.*

no matter how different, must have. That common language is science and mathematics," Sagan says. Because the laws of science and mathematics are the same throughout the universe, Sagan believes extraterrestrials will code their messages in scientific and mathematical terms.

Receipt of such messages, he says, will have an immediate payoff. For the first time, human beings could see things from a truly alien perspective. "They would view the universe somewhat differently," he says. "They would have different arts and social functions. They would be interested in things we never thought of. By comparing our knowledge with theirs, we would grow immeasurably."

Sagan points out that our own galaxy, over 100,000 light-years across and filled with hundreds of billions of stars, is old enough for intelligent life to have evolved on a multitude of worlds. He suggests that an empire of older civilizations exists, and in its possession is an "Encyclopedia Galactica," a guide to all the civilizations in the galaxy. Someday, Sagan believes, earth's inhabitants will join the community of civilizations listed in that encyclopedia.

6
Detecting Signals from Space: What Will We Do?

EVER SINCE THE public reacted in panic to Orson Welles's "War of the Worlds" broadcast, government officials and the scientific community have worried about how the public would respond to news of extraterrestrial contact. Humanity is probably not much better prepared now than it was then when it comes to dealing with an alien civilization. Word of an extraterrestrial spacecraft landing either on earth or a nearby planet probably would stir a great deal of apprehension, even today.

But most scientists agree that detection of a signal from an extraterrestrial civilization on some distant world would not cause the kind of panic that arose during the now-famous radio broadcast. And, because of the huge distances between stars, detection of a signal is more likely, many scientists believe, than an actual landing. Nevertheless, many scientists working in the field of extraterrestrial research say more preparation is needed before contact is made—whether through a distant radio signal or an actual landing.

Michael Michaud, director of the Office of Ad-

(opposite page) The chances of detecting a signal from another civilization are greater than making actual contact, many scientists believe.

vanced Technology at the U.S. Department of State, is among those who express concern about the lack of preparation. "We have not created the philosophical context or the institutional framework for a calm and rational relationship with aliens," Michaud says.

Most scientists agree that some kind of preparation is needed. Whether it is by radio signal or direct contact, the revelation of an alien civilization is bound to profoundly affect people everywhere. Preparation would allow human beings to react in a civilized and dignified manner, a manner that would be appropriate for one of the great events in human history.

For exactly this reason, SETI scientists have worked hard to establish a set of procedures, or protocols, for handling the detection of extrater-

"HOWDY STRANGER!"

restrial signals. Many versions of these protocols were drafted over the past decade, but two have emerged as the procedures most likely to be followed. The first is an international protocol known as the Declaration of Principles Concerning Activities Following the Detection of Extraterrestrial Intelligence. The second is NASA's SETI Microwave Observing Project Post Detection Protocol.

Both represent agreements between SETI scientists and scientific research organizations around the world. The agreements have no diplomatic or governmental status. In fact, as of this writing, there are no protocols between governments regarding what to do if a signal is detected. This is generally not seen as a problem, however, because it is mostly scientific organizations, not governments, conducting the searches for extraterrestrial beings.

The Declaration of Principles

The international Declaration of Principles first requires the organization discovering the signal to verify that it is extraterrestrial. The declaration outlines a series of steps including a check of computer system software to confirm authenticity. This is done to avoid the false alarms that have plagued researchers in the past. Once the discovery is confirmed, all other protocol participants must be notified of the discovery. Then news of the discovery should be passed on to the International Astronomical Union, an affiliation of professional astronomers, to the United Nations, and to international research organizations. This is done in an effort to share any discoveries with other scientists and to make the discovery a world event.

The declaration suggests this information must be promptly and openly distributed to scientific and public information sources, including journals, newspapers, magazines, and radio and television news reporters. In other words, the information will be made available to citizens of the entire world. The discoverer would be entitled to make the first public announcement.

The Declaration of Principles also designates procedures for scientific study and analysis of any information contained in the signal. Such information might include facts about the biological structure of the aliens or new scientific information. A special committee of scientists would answer questions from the public about the information contained in the signal. This is done to ensure that no one group or nation conceals the discovery in order to gain a scientific or technological advantage over others.

The declaration also outlines procedures for responding to a signal from an extraterrestrial civilization. To avoid any one nation trying to set response policy for the whole world, it requires that no communications be sent until international consultations between scientists and world leaders have occurred. This international group would decide the content of the response or decide if we should respond at all. To maintain a civilized stance, the response must be peaceful, offering cooperation and friendship to those who sent the signal, and indicate a respect for any differences between earth's population and the alien civilization.

Drafting a response

Human security and well-being is to be a factor in drafting a response. If the extraterrestrials seem to pose a threat, then we may choose not to respond at all. Most scientists do not really expect security to be a problem, though. The distances between stars are so great that even a civilization able to send and receive radio signals probably would not be able to travel quickly to earth.

When NASA began planning its own SETI project, the organization formed its own protocol. Like the Declaration of Principles, NASA's SETI Microwave Observing Project Post Detection Protocol also requires that the discovering party make a prompt and accurate announcement.

And similarly, the protocol requires that scientists verify the signal is genuine before any announcements are made. They will do this by using automated verification procedures built into the computer system. These programming procedures would rule out signals that might be caused by radio interference, equipment malfunction, and human-made space vehicles. A lock-on pro-

Scientists with NASA's SETI project will ensure a signal is genuine before announcing that contact with another civilization has been made. The line on this screen, for example, comes not from an alien transmission but from Pioneer 10.

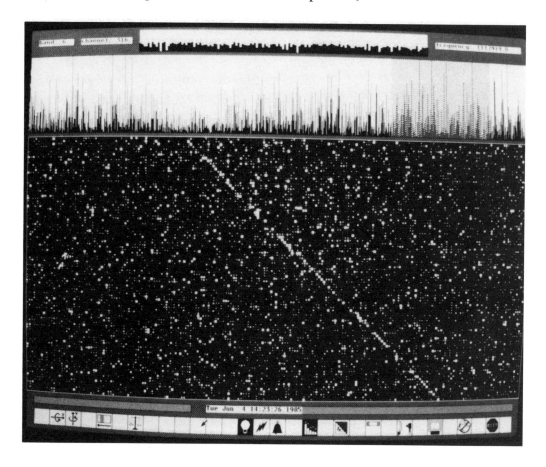

cedure will hold onto the signal as the earth rotates. This is important because many signals now detected by radio telescopes are lost as the earth rotates. The procedure will give scientists a better chance to determine the nature and source of the signal. Then, the discovery team will tell the SETI office of the signal. The office will then ask other radio observatories to locate the signal. Finally, a new set of computer programs will be loaded during the next observation period. This will help confirm that the signal was not caused by a glitch in the original computer program. Then, if the signal is confirmed to be of intelligent origin, the SETI team will tell NASA headquarters. NASA will then pass the discovery on to the president, Congress, and the news media. The organization hopes these procedures will prevent any embarrassments over false alarms.

Publishing the information

Scientific and technical information gained from the message is to be published in scientific and popular publications as soon as possible. Ongoing recording and analysis of the signal would be conducted by an expanded international team of scientists selected by the governments of participating countries. In this way, according to the protocol, "message content of the signal becomes the property of the world." Drafters of this protocol felt that the discovery of life on other worlds is simply too important to conceal from the citizens of the world. And since there is no one government that speaks for the earth anyway, the message essentially belongs to everyone.

Jill Tarter, one of those active in drafting the protocols, is nonetheless concerned that despite the protocols, information contained in the message might be withheld by a particular nation in the hopes of gaining an advantage over other na-

tions. She therefore stresses the importance of immediate and complete release of all information related to the discovery. However, she does not feel that any attempted suppression of information would last long. "I don't think it's going to be possible, simply because of the way scientists work. You're going to want to go to someone independent and get confirmation, using a completely different set of equipment. At that point, it becomes impossible to suppress anything. . . . As soon as you have to go outside your own organization, that's the beginning of the leakage process."

To help prepare people for the idea of extraterrestrial contact and to educate the public about the NASA SETI project, the space agency is forming a special outreach program. Among its goals

Jill Tarter, one of the drafters of the protocols, stresses the importance of releasing any information relating to the discovery of extraterrestrials.

"Well, don't just sit there. Run and get your camera."

would be informing people of the possible effects of contact, such as changes in our thinking about philosophy, religion, and social structure, and encouraging people to get involved by offering their opinions on what to do in event of contact.

The search for extraterrestrial life probably represents the scientific adventure of our time. There is a degree of suspense to the whole project because no one knows what is going to happen. If we discover an alien civilization, we will answer the age-old question in an exciting and exhilarating manner. But even if we discover that we are the only intelligent beings in the universe, the discovery would still be meaningful. "It would speak eloquently of how rare are the living beings of our planet and would underscore, as nothing else in human history has, the individual worth of every human being," says Sagan.

Most scientists feel the search is well worth the

effort. At hand is a universe that seems to be beckoning, calling us toward its many secrets and mysteries. We do not know what we will find at any step along the way. We can only find out what is there by searching the skies. "Nobody on earth truly knows whether we're alone or if the universe is buzzing with life," says Thomas McDonough. "Sticking our heads in the ground never got us anywhere in science. If we don't search, we'll never find anything. If we do search, the least we'll do is explore the universe."

Glossary

astronomy: The study of the heavens, including stars, planets, galaxies, and other natural objects in space.

atmosphere: A covering of gas or air surrounding a planet whose gravity is strong enough to retain it.

atom: Any of the tiny particles of which the chemical elements are made.

bandwidth: A signal that is broadcast or received over a restricted range of frequencies.

bioastronomy: The branch of astronomy that studies the possible structure of life on other worlds.

black hole: A mysterious well of gravity so powerful that everything that enters it, including light, is trapped inside.

CETI: Communication (or Contact) with ExtraTerrestrial Intelligence. This is an alternate term for SETI.

electromagnetic spectrum: The full range of energy wavelengths emitted by objects in space and by human activity on earth. This range includes radio/television waves, microwaves, infrared radiation, visible light, ultraviolet radiation, X rays, and gamma rays.

evolution: Change over a period of time, sometimes from one form to another. Biological evolution refers to adaptive changes in plants and animals over thousands or millions of years. Evolution also occurs in natural objects, however, such as stars and planets. Here, various physical laws govern changes that take place over periods up to billions of years.

exobiology: The study of possible life on other worlds.

extraterrestrial: Outside the earth or its atmosphere. In exobiology, this refers to objects in space (stars, planets, etc.) or beings from another world.

frequency: The number of cycles or oscillations of a wave motion per second.

galaxy: A large, rotating group of stars bound together by gravity. Most galaxies are millions of light-years in diameter.

geocentric: A concept of the universe that places the earth at its center with the sun, moon, and stars all revolving around the earth.

gravity: A fundamental force of nature; the force of attraction existing between all matter.

heliocentric: A concept of the universe that places the sun at its center with the earth, moon, and stars revolving around the sun.

light-year: The distance that light and other forms of electromagnetic radiation travel in one year at 186,000 miles per second. This is equal to about 5.9 million miles.

metabolism: The processing of matter and energy in living things.

molecule: The smallest particle of a substance that retain all the properties of the substance and is composed of atoms.

multichannel spectrum analyzer (also multichannel spectrometer): A computer-aided receiver that analyzes signals at different frequency ranges simultaneously.

photosynthesis: A process by which plants convert the sun's energy to oxygen and nutrients.

planet: A world circling a star that reflects rather than gives off light.

pulsar: A rapidly rotating or pulsating star that produces a burst of radio waves with each rotation.

quasar: Any of various celestial objects that resemble stars but are apparently far more distant and emit powerful radio waves.

radio astronomy: The study of radio waves produced by objects in space. This is usually done with radio dish antennas and receivers.

radio telescope: An antenna system that collects radio signals. It can also broadcast radio signals outward.

radio wave: A form of electromagnetic energy traveling at the speed of light.

SETI: The Search for ExtraTerrestrial Intelligence.

solar system: A system of planets and other bodies revolving around a star. Besides planets, our own solar system includes asteroids, comets, and cosmic dust.

star: A heavenly body such as the sun that radiates energy, including light, by nuclear reactions in its interior.

thermally habitable: Of suitable temperature for life.

UFO: An Unidentified Flying Object or a strange and unexplained object.

universe: All creation. This includes interstellar gas and dust, planets, stars, quasars, pulsars, galaxies, and the space in between.

water hole: A band of frequencies in an area of the electromagnetic spectrum that is relatively free of radio interference. It is between the frequencies of hydrogen and hydroxyl, the components of water. It is considered a likely range in which to find signals from extraterrestrials.

xenology: The study of alien life-forms.

Organizations to Contact

The following organizations are active in the search for extraterrestrial life and could provide information to interested readers.

Department of Anthropology
Cabrillo College
Aptos, CA 95003

This organization conducts conferences dedicated to preparing people for eventual contact with extraterrestrials. Participants include scientists, aerospace experts, social scientists, and science fiction authors.

International Astronomical Union Commission 51
(Bioastronomy: Search for Extraterrestrial Life)
c/o Department of Astronomy, Boston University
Boston, MA 02215

This commission consists of hundreds of member astronomers devoted to searching for life and intelligence in the universe.

JPL SETI Office
Mail Code 264-802
Jet Propulsion Laboratory
4800 Oak Grove Drive
Pasadena, CA 91109

The Jet Propulsion Laboratory is part of the NASA SETI project.

NASA SETI Project
The Ames SETI Office
Mail Code 229-8
NASA Ames Research Center
Moffett Field, CA 94035

This is the headquarters of the NASA SETI project scheduled to start in 1992.

The Planetary Society
65 North Catalina Avenue
Pasadena, CA 91106

This space-advocacy organization was cofounded by Dr. Carl Sagan. Besides vigorously promoting SETI, the organization is conducting its own SETI project.

The SETI Institute
2035 Landings Drive
Mountain View, CA 94043

This is a private, nonprofit organization headed by Dr. Frank Drake. The SETI Institute is helping NASA in the planning and operation of its SETI project.

Suggestions for Further Reading

Franklyn M. Branley, *Is There Life in Outer Space?* New York: Crowell Junior Books, 1984.

Keay Davidson, "E.T., Phone Earth," *Science Digest*, March 1989.

Don Dwiggins, *Hello? Who's Out There?* New York: Dodd, Mead, 1987.

Robert Jastrow, *Journey to the Stars: Space Exploration—Tomorrow and Beyond.* New York: Bantam Books, 1989.

Michael D. Lemonick, "Is Anybody Out There?" *Science Digest*, October 1985.

Margaret Poynter and Michael J. Klein, *Cosmic Quest: Searching for Intelligent Life Among the Stars.* New York: Atheneum Publishers, 1984.

Carl Sagan, *Other Worlds.* New York: Bantam Books, 1975.

Bruce Schechter, "Combing the Cosmic Haystack," *Discover*, March 1983.

Geraldine Woods and Harold Woods, *Is There Life on Other Planets?* New York: EMC Corporation, 1980.

Works Consulted

Joseph A. Angelo, Jr., *The Extraterrestrial Encyclopedia.* New York: Facts on File, 1985.

Isaac Asimov, *Extraterrestrial Civilizations.* New York: Crown, 1979.

Richard Berendzen, ed., *Life Beyond Earth & the Mind of Man.* Washington, D.C.: National Aeronautics and Space Administration/U.S. Government Printing Office, 1973. NASA SP-328.

Ben Bova and Byron Preiss, eds., *First Contact: The Search for Extraterrestrial Intelligence.* New York: NAL Books, 1990.

Ronald Bracewell, *The Galactic Club: Intelligent Life in Outer Space.* San Francisco: W.H. Freeman, 1975.

James L. Christian, ed., *Extraterrestrial Intelligence: The First Encounter.* Buffalo: Prometheus Books, 1976.

Neil F. Comins, "Life Near the Center of the Galaxy," *Astronomy*, April 1991.

Ken Croswell, "Does Alpha Centauri Have Intelligent Life?" *Astronomy*, April 1991.

Edward Edelson, *Who Goes There? The Search for Intelligent Life in the Universe.* New York: Doubleday, 1979.

Zen Faulkes, "Getting Smart About Getting Smarts: Evolutionary Biology and Extraterrestrial Intelligence," *Skeptical Inquirer*, Spring 1991.

Gerald Feinberg and Robert Shapiro, *Life Beyond Earth: The Intelligent Earthling's Guide to Life in the Universe.* New York: William Morrow, 1980.

Donald Goldsmith, ed., *The Quest for Extraterrestrial Life: A Book of Readings.* Mill Valley, CA: University Science Books, 1980.

Richard C. Hoagland, *The Monuments of Mars: A City on the Edge of Forever.* Berkeley, CA: North Atlantic Books, 1987.

Barry Karr and Thomas R. McDonough, "Searching for Extraterrestrial Intelligence: An Interview with Thomas R. McDonough," *Skeptical Inquirer*, Spring 1991.

Magoroh Maruyama and Arthur Harkins, eds., *Cultures Beyond the Earth: The Role of Anthropology in Outer Space.* New York: Vintage Books, 1975.

Thomas R. McDonough, *The Search for Extraterrestrial Intelligence: Listening for Life in the Cosmos.* New York: John Wiley & Sons, 1986.

Kevin McKean, "Life on a Young Planet," *Discover*, March 1983.

Philip Morrison, John Billingham, and John Wolfe, eds., *The Search for Extraterrestrial Intelligence: SETI.* Washington, D.C.: National Aeronautics and Space Administration/U.S. Government Printing Office, 1977. NASA SP-419.

Edward Regis, Jr., ed., *Extraterrestrials: Science and Alien Intelligence.* New York: Cambridge University Press, 1985.

Ian Ridpath, *Messages from the Stars: Communication and Contact with Extraterrestrial Life.* New York: Harper & Row, 1978.

Robert T. Rood and James S. Trefil, *Are We Alone? The Possibility of Extraterrestrial Civilizations.* New York: Charles Scribners Sons, 1981.

Carl Sagan, *The Cosmic Connection: An Extraterrestrial Perspective.* New York: Doubleday, 1973/Dell Publishing, 1975.

Carl Sagan, *Cosmos.* New York: Random House, 1980.

Carl Sagan, "We Are Nothing Special," *Discover,* March 1983.

Carl Sagan and Frank Drake, "The Search for Extraterrestrial Intelligence," *Scientific American Special Issue Exploring Space,* 1990.

Carl Sagan, ed., *Communication with Extraterrestrial Intelligence (CETI).* Cambridge, MA: The Massachusetts Institute of Technology Press, 1973.

I.S. Shklovskii and Carl Sagan, *Intelligent Life in the Universe.* San Francisco: Holden-Day, 1966/Dell Publishing, 1968.

David W. Swift, *SETI Pioneers. Scientists Talk About Their Search for Extraterrestrial Intelligence.* Tucson: The University of Arizona Press, 1990.

Jill Tarter, "Searching for THEM: Interstellar Communications," *Astronomy*, October 1982.

Frank Tipler, "We Are Alone," *Discover*, March 1983.

Shawna Vogel, "E.T., Phone NASA," *Discover,* October 1987.

Frank White, *The SETI Factor.* New York: Walker, 1990.

John Noble Wilford, *Mars Beckons.* New York: Alfred Knopf, 1990.

Index

About the Author

Richard Michael Rasmussen is a professional writer and a social service analyst with the county of San Diego. Rasmussen holds an AA degree in social science from Grossmont College and a certificate in technical writing. He is the author of one other book published by Lucent Books, *The UFO Challenge*. Rasmussen is also the author of *The UFO Literature*, published by McFarland and Company. He is a member of The Planetary Society, a space-advocacy group and, as a member of the national Society of Children's Book Writers and the San Diego Writers and Editors Guild, he gives talks at elementary and junior high schools in hopes of inspiring young people to become professional writers.

Picture Credits